I0069073

Accounting for Income Taxes

Steven M. Bragg

AccountingTools®

Copyright © 2025 by AccountingTools, Inc. All rights reserved.

Published by AccountingTools, Inc., Centennial, Colorado.

No part of this publication may be reproduced, stored in a retrieval system, or transmitted in any form or by any means, except as permitted under Section 107 or 108 of the 1976 United States Copyright Act, without the prior written permission of the Publisher. Requests to the Publisher for permission should be addressed to Steven M. Bragg, 6727 E. Fremont Place, Centennial, CO 80112.

Limit of Liability/Disclaimer of Warranty: While the publisher and author have used their best efforts in preparing this book, they make no representations or warranties with respect to the accuracy or completeness of the contents of this book and specifically disclaim any implied warranties of merchantability or fitness for a particular purpose. No warranty may be created or extended by written sales materials. The advice and strategies contained herein may not be suitable for your situation. You should consult with a professional where appropriate. Neither the publisher nor author shall be liable for any loss of profit or any other commercial damages, including but not limited to special, incidental, consequential, or other damages.

ISBN 978-1-64221-256-3

For more information about AccountingTools® products, visit our Web site at www.accountingtools.com.

Table of Contents

About the Author

Steven Bragg, CPA, has been the chief financial officer or controller of four companies, as well as a consulting manager at Ernst & Young. He received a master's degree in finance from Bentley College, an MBA from Babson College, and a Bachelor's degree in Economics from the University of Maine. He has been a two-time president of the Colorado Mountain Club, and is an avid alpine skier, mountain biker, and certified master diver. Mr. Bragg resides in Centennial, Colorado. He has written more than 300 books and courses, including *New Controller Guidebook*, *GAAP Guidebook*, and *Payroll Management*. He has also written *The Auditors* science fiction trilogy.

Steven maintains the accountingtools.com web site, which contains continuing professional education courses, the Accounting Best Practices podcast, and thousands of articles on accounting subjects.

Buy Additional AccountingTools Courses

AccountingTools offers more than 1,500 hours of CPE courses, with concentrations in accounting, auditing, finance, taxation, and ethics. Related courses that you might like include:

- Closing the Books
- Small Business Tax Guide
- The Income Statement

Go to accountingtools.com/cpe to view these additional courses.

AccountingTools®

Accounting for Income Taxes

Introduction

If a company generates a profit, it will probably be necessary to record income tax expense that is a percentage of the profit. However, the calculation of income tax is not so simple, since it may be based on a number of adjustments to net income that are allowed by the taxing authorities. The result can be remarkably complex tax measurements. In this manual, we describe the general concepts of income tax accounting, as well as the calculation of the appropriate tax rate, the evaluation of tax positions, how to treat deferred taxes, the taxation of undistributed earnings, how to record taxes in interim periods, and other related topics. The guidance in this manual applies to United States federal income taxes for United States entities, as well as to foreign, state, and local taxes that are based on income.

Overview of Income Taxes

Before delving into the income taxes topic, we must clarify several concepts that are essential to understanding the related accounting. The concepts are:

- *Temporary differences.* A company may record an asset or liability at one value for financial reporting purposes, while maintaining a separate record of a different value for tax purposes. The difference is caused by the tax recognition policies of taxing authorities, who may require the deferral or acceleration of certain items for tax reporting purposes. These differences are temporary, since the assets will eventually be recovered and the liabilities settled, at which point the differences will be terminated. A difference that results in a taxable amount in a later period is called a *taxable temporary difference*, while a difference that results in a deductible amount in a later period is called a *deductible temporary difference*. Examples of temporary differences are:
  - o Revenues or gains that are taxable either prior to or after they are recognized in the financial statements. For example, an allowance for doubtful accounts may not be immediately tax deductible, but instead must be deferred until specific receivables are declared bad debts.
  - o Expenses or losses that are tax deductible either prior to or after they are recognized in the financial statements. For example, some fixed assets are tax deductible at once, but can only be recognized through long-term depreciation in the financial statements. As another example, organizational costs are charged to expense as incurred for financial reporting purposes, but are deferred and deducted in a later year for tax purposes.
  - o Assets whose tax basis is reduced by investment tax credits.

1

EXAMPLE

In its most recent year of operations, Table Furniture earns $250,000. Table also has $30,000 of taxable temporary differences and $80,000 of deductible temporary differences. Based on this information, Table's taxable income in the current year is calculated as:

$250,000 Profit - $30,000 Taxable temporary differences
+ $80,000 Deductible temporary differences

= $300,000 Taxable profit

- *Carrybacks and carryforwards.* A company may find that it has more tax deductions or tax credits (from an operating loss) than it can use in the current year's tax return. If so, it has the option of offsetting these amounts against the taxable income or tax liabilities (respectively) of the tax returns in earlier periods, or in future periods. Carrying these amounts back to the tax returns of prior periods is always more valuable, since the company can apply for a tax refund at once, and recognize a receivable for the amount of the refund. Thus, these excess tax deductions or tax credits are carried back first, with any remaining amounts being reserved for use in future periods. Carryforwards eventually expire, if not used within a certain number of years. A company should recognize a receivable for the amount of taxes paid in prior years that are refundable due to a carryback. A deferred tax asset can be realized for a carryforward, but possibly with an offsetting valuation allowance that is based on the probability that some portion of the carryforward will not be realized.

EXAMPLE

Spastic Corporation has created $100,000 of deferred tax assets through the diligent generation of losses for the past five years. Based on the company's poor competitive stance, management believes it is more likely than not that there will be inadequate profits (if any) against which the deferred tax assets can be offset. Accordingly, Spastic recognizes a valuation allowance in the amount of $100,000 that fully offsets the deferred tax assets.

- *Deferred tax liabilities and assets.* When there are temporary differences, the result can be deferred tax assets and deferred tax liabilities, which represent the change in taxes payable or refundable in future periods.

EXAMPLE

Armadillo Industries elects to account for a government contract on the percentage of completion method for financial reporting purposes, and on the completed contract method for tax reporting purposes. By doing so, the company recognizes income in its financial statements throughout the term of the contract, but does not do so for tax reporting purposes until the end of the contract.

EXAMPLE

Uncanny Corporation has recorded the following carrying amount and tax basis information for certain of its assets and liabilities:

(000s)	Carrying Amount	Tax Basis	Temporary Difference
Accounts receivable	$12,000	$12,250	-$250
Prepaid expenses	350	350	0
Inventory	8,000	8,400	-400
Fixed assets	17,300	14,900	2,400
Accounts payable	3,700	3,700	0
Totals	$41,350	$39,600	$1,750

In the table, Uncanny has included a reserve for bad debts in its accounts receivable figure and for obsolete inventory in its inventory number, neither of which are allowed for tax purposes. Also, the company applied an accelerated form of depreciation to its fixed assets for tax purposes and straight-line depreciation for its financial reporting. These three items account for the total temporary difference between the carrying amount and tax basis of the items shown in the table.

All of these factors can result in complex calculations to arrive at the appropriate income tax information to recognize and report in the financial statements.

Accounting for Income Taxes

Despite the complexity inherent in income taxes, the essential accounting in this area is derived from the need to recognize just two items, which are:

- *Current year.* The recognition of a tax liability or tax asset, based on the estimated amount of income taxes payable or refundable for the current year.
- *Future years.* The recognition of a deferred tax liability or tax asset, based on the estimated effects in future years of carryforwards and temporary differences.

Based on the preceding points, the general accounting for income taxes is as follows:

+/-	Create a tax liability for estimated taxes payable, and/or create a tax asset for tax refunds, that relate to the current or prior years
+/-	Create a deferred tax liability for estimated future taxes payable, and/or create a deferred tax asset for estimated future tax refunds, that can be attributed to temporary differences and carryforwards
=	Total income tax expense in the period

Tax Positions

A tax position is a stance taken by a company in its tax return that measures tax assets and liabilities, and which results in the permanent reduction or temporary deferral of income taxes. When constructing the proper accounting for a tax position, the accountant follows these steps:

1. Evaluate whether the tax position taken has merit, based on the tax regulations.
2. If the tax position has merit, measure the amount that can be recognized in the financial statements.
3. Determine the probability and amount of settlement with the taxing authorities. Recognition should only be made when it is more likely than not (i.e., more than 50% probability) that the company's tax position will be sustained once it has been examined by the governing tax authorities. This probability is based on the facts, circumstances, and information available at the reporting date.
4. Recognize the tax position, if warranted.

Tip: Given the large financial impact of some tax positions, it makes sense to obtain an outside opinion of a proposed position by a tax expert, and document the results of that review thoroughly. This is helpful not only if the position is reviewed by the taxing authorities, but also when it is reviewed by the company's outside auditors.

EXAMPLE

Armadillo Industries takes a tax position on an issue and determines that the position qualifies for recognition, and so should be recognized. The following table shows the estimated possible outcomes of the tax position, along with their associated probabilities:

Possible Outcome	Probability of Occurrence	Cumulative Probability
$250,000	5%	5%
200,000	20%	25%
150,000	40%	65%
100,000	20%	85%
50,000	10%	95%
0	5%	100%

Since the benefit amount just beyond the 50% threshold level is $150,000, Armadillo should recognize a tax benefit of $150,000.

If a company initially concludes that the probability of a tax position being sustained is less than 50%, it should not initially recognize the tax position. However, it can recognize the position at a later date if the probability increases to be in excess of 50%, or if the tax position is settled through interaction with the taxing authorities, or the statute of limitations keeps the taxing authorities from challenging the tax position. If a company subsequently concludes that it will change a tax position previously taken, it should recognize the effect of the change in the period in which it alters its tax position. A change in tax position should be based on the evaluation of new information, rather than from a new evaluation of information that was available in an earlier reporting period.

EXAMPLE

Armadillo Industries takes a tax position under which it accelerates the depreciation of certain production equipment well beyond the normally-allowed taxable rate, resulting in a deferred tax liability after three years of $120,000.

After three years, a tax court ruling convinces Armadillo management that its tax position is untenable. Consequently, the company recognizes a tax liability for the $120,000 temporary difference. At the company's current 20% tax rate, this results in increased taxes of $24,000 and the elimination of the temporary difference.

A business may conclude that a tax position has been effectively settled following its examination by the relevant taxing authority. The assessment of whether such settlement has occurred depends upon consideration of *all* of the following conditions:

- The taxing authority has finalized its examination procedures, including all administrative reviews and appeals.
- The company does not intend to appeal any part of its tax position or engage in litigation.
- The probability that the taxing authority would examine any aspect of the tax position is remote, based on its policy for reopening closed examinations and the facts and circumstances related to the tax position.

A business should derecognize a tax position that it had previously recognized if the probability of the tax position being sustained drops below 50%, based on the most recent facts and circumstances.

If there is a change in the tax laws or tax rates, a business cannot recognize alterations in its income tax liability in advance of the enactment of these laws and rates. Instead, the company must wait until enactment has been completed, and can then recognize the changes on the enactment date.

Deferred Tax Expense

Deferred tax expense is the net change in the deferred tax liabilities and assets of a business during a period of time. The amount of deferred taxes should be compiled for each tax-paying component of a business that provides a consolidated tax return. Doing so requires that the business complete the following steps:

1. Identify the existing temporary differences and carryforwards.
2. Determine the deferred tax liability amount for those temporary differences that are taxable, using the applicable tax rate.
3. Determine the deferred tax asset amount for those temporary differences that are deductible, as well as any operating loss carryforwards, using the applicable tax rate.
4. Determine the deferred tax asset amount for any carryforwards involving tax credits.
5. Create a valuation allowance for the deferred tax assets if there is a more than 50% probability that the company will not realize some portion of these assets. Any changes to this allowance are to be recorded within income from continuing operations on the income statement. The need for a valuation allowance is especially likely if a business has a history of letting various carryforwards expire unused, or it expects to incur losses in the next few years. A cumulative loss in recent years is a strong indicator that a valuation allowance is needed. A business should consider its tax planning strategy when determining the amount of a valuation allowance.

A valuation allowance may not be needed when there is positive evidence to support a deferred tax asset. For example:

- The company has a large sales backlog and sufficient production capacity to ensure that it can produce a sufficient amount of taxable income.
- The company has a sufficiently large amount of appreciated asset value to generate taxable income.
- The company has a strong track record of profitability, along with evidence indicating that the loss triggering the deferred tax asset is likely to be an aberration.

Applicable Tax Rate

In general, when measuring a deferred tax liability or asset, a business should use the tax rate that it expects to apply to the taxable income that results from the realization of deferred tax assets or settlement of deferred tax liabilities. Also consider the following issues:

- *Alternative minimum tax.* The alternative minimum tax may increase the effective tax rate used. It may be necessary to reduce the deferred tax asset for the alternative minimum tax credit carryforward with a valuation allowance, if it is more than 50% probable that the asset will not be realized.
- *Discounting.* Deferred taxes are not to be discounted to their present value when they are recognized.
- *Graduated tax rates.* If the applicable tax law has graduated tax rates, and the graduated rates significantly affect the average tax rate paid, use the average tax rate that applies to the estimated annual taxable income in those periods when deferred tax liabilities are settled or deferred tax assets are realized. If a company earns such a large amount of income that the graduated rate is not significantly different from the top-tier tax rate, use the top-tier rate for the estimation of annual taxable income.
- *New tax laws or rates.* A company should adjust the amount of its deferred tax liabilities and assets for the effect of any changes in tax laws or tax rates, which shall be recorded within income from continuing operations. Doing so may also call for an adjustment to the related valuation allowance. The effect of these changes should be recognized on the date when they are enacted.

Interest and Penalties

When there is a requirement in the tax law that interest be paid when income taxes are not fully paid, a company should begin recognizing the amount of this interest expense as soon as the expense would be scheduled to begin accruing under the tax law.

If a company takes a tax position that will incur penalties, it should recognize the related penalty expense as soon as the company takes the position in a tax return. Whether penalties should be recognized may depend on management's judgment of whether a tax position exceeds the minimum statutory threshold required to avoid the payment of a penalty.

If a tax position is eventually sustained, reverse in the current period any related interest and penalties that had been accrued in previous periods under the expectation that the position would not be sustained.

Change in Tax Status

The tax status of a business may change from taxable to nontaxable, or vice versa. For example, a partnership may convert into a corporation, thereby changing from a non-taxable (pass-through) entity to a taxable entity. When a nontaxable entity becomes taxable, it should recognize a deferred tax liability or asset for any outstanding temporary differences as of the conversion date. The conversion date can be either the date on which the taxing authority approves the change, or the filing date, if approval is not necessary.

When a taxable entity becomes nontaxable, all deferred tax assets and liabilities should be eliminated as of the date of this transition.

Intraperiod Tax Allocation

Intraperiod tax allocation is the allocation of income taxes to different parts of the results appearing in the income statement of a business, so that some items are stated net of tax. Income taxes are allocated among the following items:

- Continuing operations
- Discontinued operations
- Other comprehensive income
- Items assigned directly to shareholders' equity

The intraperiod tax allocation concept is used to reveal the "true" results of certain transactions net of all effects, rather than disaggregating them from income taxes. For example, a company records a gain of $1 million. Its tax rate is 21%, so the company reports the gain net of taxes, at $790,000.

When allocating income taxes among the various income statement items just noted, allocate the taxes using either of the following methodologies:

- *One allocation target.* First assign income taxes to continuing operations, and then assign all remaining income taxes to the remaining allocation target.
- *Multiple allocation targets.* First assign income taxes to continuing operations, and then assign the remaining income taxes to the other items in proportion to their individual impact on the amount of remaining income taxes.

Note that, though the income tax included in these net calculations is usually an expense, it may also be a credit, so that any of the preceding items presented net of tax would include the tax credit.

Most elements of the income statement are not presented net of the intraperiod tax allocation. For example, revenue, the cost of goods sold, and administrative expenses are not presented net of income taxes.

EXAMPLE

Uncanny Corporation earns $500,000 of income from continuing operations, and experiences a loss of $150,000 from a discontinued operation. At the beginning of the year, Uncanny had a $600,000 tax loss carryforward. Uncanny applies the tax loss carryforward against the $500,000 income from continuing operations. Since the offset eliminates the $500,000 of income from operations, no income tax is applied to it. The company then applies the remaining $100,000 of tax loss carryforward against the loss from a discontinued operation, leaving $50,000 of taxable loss to be reported for the discontinued operation.

Taxes Related to Undistributed Earnings

There are a few instances where a business is not required to engage in the standard accounting and disclosure of deferred income taxes for temporary differences. These exceptions relate to investments in subsidiaries and corporate joint ventures, and whether they remit earnings to the corporate parent or investors, respectively.

A corporate subsidiary typically remits earnings to the parent entity only after a number of issues have been considered, such as the need for cash by the subsidiary and parent, tax issues, and creditor and government restrictions. Funds may be remitted from a corporate joint venture based on the payout clauses in the original joint venture agreement, or with the agreement of the investing parties. In many situations, no funds are remitted, or only a small portion of the full amount of earnings.

Generally, the accounting for these undistributed earnings is to include them in the earnings of the parent entity, which results in a temporary difference, unless there is a means by which an investment in a domestic subsidiary can be recovered, free of tax. The same accounting approach applies to the pretax income of corporate joint ventures that are unlikely to be remitted to investors, and where the investors account for their investments in the joint ventures with the equity method.

A corporate joint venture may have a limited life span that will likely trigger the release of undistributed earnings to investors at the end of that lifespan. If so, investors should record deferred taxes when the profits or losses of the venture are recorded in its financial statements.

An investor entity should record a deferred tax liability when there is an excess of the reported taxable temporary difference over the tax basis:

- Of an investment in a domestic subsidiary
- In an investee that is ≤ 50% owned

A temporary difference is not considered a taxable temporary difference when there is a method permitted under the tax law for recovering the amount of an investment tax-free, *and* the investing entity expects to use that method. For example, it is possible to do so under certain types of acquisition structures, such as when a subsidiary is merged into the parent company, with noncontrolling shareholders receiving the stock of the parent company in exchange for their shares in the subsidiary.

When there is an excess of tax basis for an investment in a subsidiary or joint venture over the amount recorded in the financial statements, and the temporary difference will reverse in the foreseeable future, the corporate parent or investor should recognize a deferred tax asset in the amount of the difference. For example, the decision to sell a subsidiary would make it likely that a temporary difference will reverse in the near future.

The tax benefit associated with a deferred tax asset should be recognized when it is more than 50% probable that the temporary difference will reverse in the foreseeable future. Similarly, a tax expense should be recognized when it is more than 50% probable that a deferred tax liability will reverse in the foreseeable future.

It may be necessary to create a valuation allowance that will offset a deferred tax asset. The amount of this allowance (if any) shall be based on a periodic assessment of the allowance.

The parent entity should *not* accrue income taxes for unremitted earnings only in those situations where a subsidiary will permanently retain its earnings (which requires a reinvestment plan), or where the remittance will involve a tax-free liquidation. If circumstances change, and it appears that some portion of a subsidiary's undistributed earnings will be remitted, the parent should accrue income taxes related to the amount that will be remitted. If the reverse situation arises, where it no longer appears likely that earnings will be remitted, reduce the amount of income tax expense that had been previously recognized.

Interim Reporting

If a business reports its financial results during interim reporting periods (such as monthly or quarterly financial statements), it must report income taxes in those interim reports. In general, the proper accounting is to report income taxes using an estimated effective tax rate in all of the interim periods. However, the application of this general principle varies somewhat as noted below:

- *Ordinary income.* Calculate the income tax on ordinary income at the estimated annual effective tax rate.
- *Other items.* Calculate and recognize the income tax on all items other than ordinary income at the rates that are applicable when the items occur. This means that the related tax effect is recognized in the period in which the underlying items occur.

The following factors apply to the determination of the estimated annual effective tax rate:

- The tax benefit associated with any applicable operating loss carryforward
- The tax effect of any valuation allowance used to offset the deferred tax asset
- Anticipated investment tax credits (for the amount expected to be used within the year)
- Foreign tax rates
- Capital gains rates

Accounting for Income Taxes

- The effects of new tax legislation, though only after it has been passed
- Other applicable factors

EXAMPLE

In the current fiscal year, Armadillo Industries anticipates $1,000,000 of ordinary income, to which will be applied the statutory tax rate of 21%, which will result in an income tax expense of $210,000. Armadillo also expects to take advantage of a $100,000 investment tax credit. Thus, the effective tax rate for the year is expected to be 11%, which is calculated as $110,000 of net taxes, divided by $1,000,000 of ordinary income.

Do not include in the determination of the estimated annual effective tax rate the effect of taxes related to unusual or discontinued operations that are expected to be reported separately in the financial statements.

The estimated tax rate is to be reviewed at the end of each interim period and adjusted as necessary, based on the latest estimates of taxable income to be reported for the full year. If it is not possible to derive an estimated tax rate, it may be necessary to instead use the actual effective tax rate for the year to date.

If the estimated tax rate is revised in an interim period from the rate used in a prior period, use the new estimate to derive the year-to-date tax on ordinary income for all interim periods to date.

The tax benefit associated with a loss recorded in an earlier interim period may not be recognized, on the grounds that it is less than 50% probable that the benefit will be realized. If so, do not recognize any income tax for ordinary income reported in subsequent periods until the unrecognized tax benefit associated with the original loss has been offset with income.

EXAMPLE

Through its first two quarters, Uncanny Corporation has experienced losses of $400,000 and $600,000. Management concludes that it is more likely than not that the tax benefit associated with these losses will not be realized. The company then earns profits in the third and fourth quarters, resulting in the following application of taxes at the statutory 21% corporate rate:

| (000s) | Ordinary Income | | Income Tax | | |
	Current Period	Cumulative	Cumulative Tax (20%)	Less Previous Amount	Tax Provision
Quarter 1	-$400	-$400	--	---	--
Quarter 2	-600	-1,000	--	---	--
Quarter 3	1,100	100	$21	---	$21
Quarter 4	300	400	84	$21	63
Totals	$400				$84

If a company records a loss during an interim period, the company should only recognize the tax effects of the loss (i.e., a corresponding reduction in taxes) when there is an expectation that the tax reduction will be realized later in the year, or will be recognized as a deferred tax asset by year-end. This recognition may occur later in the year, if it later becomes more likely than not that the tax effects of the loss can be realized.

EXAMPLE

Uncanny Corporation has a history of recording losses in its first and second quarters, after which sales increase during the summer and winter holiday seasons. In the first half of the current year, Uncanny records a $1,000,000 loss, but expects a $2,000,000 profit in the final half of the year. Based on the company's history of seasonal sales, realization of the tax loss appears to be more likely than not, so Uncanny records the tax effect of the loss in the first half of the year.

If a business is subject to a variety of tax rates because of its operations in multiple tax jurisdictions, the estimated tax rate shall be based on a single tax rate for the entire company. When developing the single company-wide tax rate, exclude the effects of ordinary losses within jurisdictions, and develop a separate estimated tax rate for those jurisdictions. Also, if it is impossible to estimate a tax rate or ordinary income in a foreign jurisdiction, exclude that jurisdiction from the computation of the company-wide tax rate.

A company may decide to record a change in accounting principle. If so, the amount of the change included in retained earnings at the beginning of the fiscal year shall include the effect of the applicable amount of tax expense or benefit, employing the tax rate used for the full fiscal year. If the change in principle is made in an interim period other than the first interim period of a fiscal year, retrospectively apply the change to the preceding interim periods in the same year; when doing so, apply the estimated tax rate that originally applied to those periods, modified for the effects of the change in principle.

Income Taxes Presentation

The following income tax issues can affect the presentation of tax information in the financial statements:

- *Deferred tax accounts.* Classify deferred tax assets and deferred tax liabilities as noncurrent amounts.
- *Interest and penalties.* Any recognized interest expense related to tax positions can be classified within either the interest expense or income taxes line items. Any penalties expense related to tax positions can be classified within either the income taxes or some other expense line items.
- *Intraperiod tax allocation.* If income taxes are being allocated among income statement line items in an interim period, allocate taxes based on the estimated

amount of annual ordinary income, plus other items that have occurred during the year to date. These other items may require income tax allocations to discontinued operations, other comprehensive income, and/or items charged to shareholders' equity.

- *Netting*. Within a tax jurisdiction for a single entity, it is permissible to net the noncurrent deferred tax assets and the noncurrent deferred tax liabilities. Do not net those deferred tax assets and deferred tax liabilities that are attributed to unrelated tax jurisdictions or components of the business.

- *Tax status*. If there is a change in the tax status of an entity, record the change within the income from continuing operations section of the income statement.

- *Undistributed earnings*. All changes in the income tax accruals related to undistributed earnings from subsidiaries and joint ventures should be recorded in the income tax expense line item.

Income Taxes Disclosure

A business should disclose the following information in its financial statements that relates to income taxes, broken down by where the information should be disclosed.

Balance Sheet

The following information about income taxes should be disclosed within the balance sheet or the accompany notes:

- *Carryforwards*. The amounts of all operating loss carryforwards and tax credit carryforwards, as well as their related expiration dates. For example:

    As of December 31, 20X5, the company had gross federal net operating loss carry forwards of approximately $1,250,000 expiring beginning in 20X9 and gross state net operating loss carry forwards of approximately $190,000 expiring beginning in 20X8.

- *Deferrals.* The total of all deferred tax liabilities, the total of all deferred tax assets, and the total valuation allowance associated with the deferred tax assets. Also disclose the net change in the valuation allowance during the year. For example:

(000s)	
Deferred tax assets (liabilities):	
Fixed assets	$1,770
Prepaid expenses	-410
Accrued stock compensation	2,780
Accrued restructuring costs	10
Work opportunity credit carryforward	5,230
Operating loss carryforward	10,660
Intangibles and goodwill	-65
Derivative instruments	-50
Cumulative translation adjustment	-965
Other	135
Net deferred tax assets	19,095
Valuation allowance	-18,940
Total net deferred tax asset	$155

- *Tax status.* A change in tax status, if the change occurred after the end of the reporting year but before the related financial statements have been issued or are available to be issued.
- *Temporary differences and carryforwards.* The types of significant temporary differences and carryforwards, if the company is not publicly-held. If the entity is publicly-held, it must also disclose the tax effect of each temporary difference and carryforward that causes a significant part of the reported deferred tax assets and liabilities.
- *Unrecognized tax benefits, offsetting of.* If there is an unrecognized tax benefit, present it as a reduction of any deferred tax assets for a tax credit carryforward, a net operating loss carryforward, or a similar tax loss. If there is no offset available, present the unrecognized tax benefit as a liability.

- *Valuation allowance.* That portion of the valuation allowance (if any) related to deferred tax assets for which recognized tax benefits are to be credited to contributed capital (such as a deductible expenditure that reduces the proceeds from a stock issuance). For example:

  > The company has recorded a $10 million deferred tax asset, which reflects the $25 million benefit to be derived from loss carryforwards. These carryforwards expire during the period 20X5 to 20X9. The realization of this tax asset is dependent upon the company generating a sufficient amount of taxable income before the loss carryforwards expire. Management believes it is more likely than not that all $10 million of the deferred tax asset will be realized.

Income Statement

The following information about income taxes should be disclosed within the income statement or the accompanying notes:

- *Comparison to statutory rate.* The nature of significant reasons why the reported income tax differs from the statutory tax rate, for a privately-held company. Also, expand the discussion to a numerical reconciliation, if the entity is publicly-held. For example:

  > Differences between U.S. federal statutory income tax rates and our effective tax rates for continuing operations were:

	20X8
U.S. statutory tax rate	21.0%
Effect of state taxes	14.4%
Foreign income taxed in the United States	-19.8%
Uncertain tax positions	75.0%
Valuation allowance	208.0%
Other permanent differences	-12.4%
Stock-based compensation	20.4%
Other, net	-0.4%
Total	19.4%

- *Interest and penalties.* The amount of interest and penalties recognized in the period. For example:

  > At December 31, 20X4, the company had approximately $195,000 accrued for interest and penalties related to unrecognized tax benefits, net of federal tax benefit.

- *Tax allocations*. The income tax amount allocated to continuing operations and to other items. For example:

(000s)	20X1
Current:	
Federal	$685
State	-50
Foreign	210
Total current expense	845
Deferred:	
Federal	320
State	-25
Foreign	40
Total deferred expense	335
Income tax expense	$1,180

- *Tax components*. The components of income taxes attributable to continuing operations, including the current tax expense, deferred tax expense, investment tax credits, government grants, benefits related to operating loss carryforwards, the tax expense resulting from the allocation of tax benefits to contributed capital, adjustments related to enacted tax laws or rates, adjustments from a change in tax status, and adjustments to the beginning valuation allowance. For example:

(000s)	
Current tax expense	$810
Deferred tax expense	1,240
Tax expense from continuing operations	$2,050
Tax expense at statutory rate	$2,250
Benefit of investment tax credits	-80
Benefit of operating loss carryforwards	-120
Tax expense from continuing operations	$2,050

Other

The following disclosures are not associated with a particular financial statement. They must be disclosed as part of the general set of financial statements.

- *Examination years.* The tax years remaining that are subject to examination by taxing authorities. For example:

  The company's U.S. federal returns and most state returns for tax years 20X5 and forward are subject to examination. Mexican returns for tax years 20X4 and forward are subject to examination.

- *Impact on tax rate.* If the entity is publicly-held, the amount of unrecognized tax benefits that would impact the effective tax rate if they were recognized.
- *Income taxes paid.* All entities should disclose on an annual basis the following information about income taxes paid:

  o The amount of income taxes paid (net of refunds received), disaggregated by federal, state, and foreign taxes.
  o The amount of income taxes paid (net of refunds received), disaggregated by individual jurisdictions in which income taxes paid (net of refunds received) is equal to or greater than five percent of total income taxes paid (net of refunds received).

- *Interim period tax variations.* If the application of accounting standards for income taxes in interim periods results in a significant variation from the usual income tax percentage, the reasons for the variation. For example:

  For the second quarter and first six months of 20X7, the company recorded a provision for income taxes of $5.1 million and an effective tax rate of 20.2%, and $9.3 million and an effective tax rate of 20.9%, respectively. The company's provision for income taxes and effective tax rate for the second quarter and first six months of 20X7 were impacted by the previously discussed restructuring, integration, and other charges, as well as a loss on the disposition of a subsidiary. Excluding the impact of these items, the company's effective tax rate for the second quarter and first six months of 20X7 was 19.3% and 19.9%, respectively.

- *Policies.* The policy for the classification of interest and penalty expenses. Also, the policy for the methods used to account for investment tax credits. For example:

  The company's policy is to reflect penalties and interest as part of income tax expense as they become applicable.

- *Tax holiday.* If the entity is publicly-held, the aggregate and per-share effect of a tax holiday, a description of the circumstances, and when the tax holiday will end. For example:

  > The company has been granted tax holidays as an incentive to attract foreign investment by the governments of Morocco, Ghana, and South Africa. Generally, a tax holiday is an agreement between the company and a foreign government under which the company receives certain tax benefits in that country. In all three countries, the company has been granted approval for an indefinite exemption from income taxes. The aggregate reduction in income tax expense for the year ended December 31, 20X2 was $3,400,000.

- *Undistributed earnings.* Whenever a deferred tax liability is not recognized, disclose the following:

  - Description of the underlying temporary differences, and what would cause them to be taxable
  - The amount related to permanent investments in foreign subsidiaries and foreign joint ventures, or a statement that the amount cannot be determined
  - The amount related to permanent investment in domestic subsidiaries and domestic joint ventures

- *Unrecognized tax benefits reconciliation.* If the entity is publicly-held, a tabular reconciliation of unrecognized tax changes during the period, including changes caused by tax positions taken in the current period and separately for the prior period, decreases based on settlements concluded, and any decreases caused by a lapse in the statute of limitations. For example:

(000s)	20X4	20X3
Balance at January 1	$5,170	$4,080
Additions based on tax positions related to the current year	880	1,530
Additions for tax positions of prior years	240	930
Reductions for tax positions of prior years	-390	-570
Settlements	-2,810	-800
Balance at December 31	$3,090	$5,170

Public Company Disclosures

A publicly-held business is required to disclose a rate reconciliation along with its other income tax disclosures, as well as additional information pertaining to reconciling items that are equal to or greater than five percent of the amount computed by multiplying pretax income by the statutory income tax rate.

The rate reconciliation for a public company must be in a tabular format, using both percentages and reporting currency amounts, in accordance with the following requirements:

1. The tabular format must include the following items:

    a. State and local income tax, net of any federal income tax effect
    b. Foreign tax effects
    c. The effect of changes in tax laws or rates enacted in the current period
    d. The effect of cross-border tax laws
    e. Tax credits
    f. Changes in valuation allowances
    g. Nontaxable or nondeductible items
    h. Changes in unrecognized tax benefits

2. Separate disclosure is required for any of the following reconciling items where its effect is equal to or greater than five percent of the amount computed by multiplying the income or loss from continuing operations before income taxes by the applicable statutory income tax rate:

    a. If the reconciling item is within the effect of cross-border tax laws, tax credits, or nontaxable or nondeductible items categories, it is required to be disaggregated by nature.
    b. If the reconciling item is within the foreign tax effects category, it is required to be disaggregated by jurisdiction and by nature, except for the reconciling items related to changes in unrecognized tax benefits discussed in (4).
    c. If the reconciling item does not fall within any of the categories listed in (1), it is required to be disaggregated by nature.

3. For the purpose of categorizing reconciling items, except for reconciling items related to changes in unrecognized tax benefits discussed in (4), the state and local income tax category should reflect income taxes imposed at the state or local level within the jurisdiction of domicile, the foreign tax effects category should reflect income taxes imposed by foreign jurisdictions, and the remaining categories listed in (1) should reflect federal income taxes imposed by the jurisdiction of domicile.

4. For the purpose of presenting reconciling items:

    a. Reconciling items are required to be presented on a gross basis with two exceptions under which unrecognized tax benefits and the related tax positions and tax effects of certain cross-border tax laws and the related tax credits may be presented on a net basis.
    b. Reconciling items presented in the changes in unrecognized tax benefits category may be disclosed on an aggregated basis for all jurisdictions.

For the state and local category, a public business entity is required to provide a qualitative description of the states and local jurisdictions that make up the majority of the effect of the state and local income tax category.

A public business entity is required to provide an explanation, if not otherwise evident, of the individual reconciling items disclosed, such as the nature, effect, and underlying causes of the reconciling items and the judgment used in categorizing the reconciling items.

Note: Entities other than public business entities should provide qualitative disclosures about specific categories of reconciling items and individual jurisdictions that result in a significant difference between the statutory tax rate and the effective tax rate.

Summary

Many accountants consider income tax accounting to be an area best left to a tax specialist, who churns through the information provided and creates a set of tax-related journal entries. While this approach should result in accurate tax accounting, it does not give management a good view of how its actions are affecting the taxes the company is paying – instead, the tax accounting function is treated as a black box whose contents are unknown to all, save the tax specialist who guards it.

A better approach is to engage the management team in tax planning by instructing them on the essential tax issues that can be impacted by strategic and tactical decisions. Even if management does not become conversant at a detailed level in how their actions impact income taxes, they will at least know when to call in a tax expert to advise them. Thus, a certain amount of transparency in the tax area can improve the results of a business.

Glossary

A

Alternative minimum tax. A tax that is derived from an alternative determination of tax liability, as stated in the U.S. Internal Revenue Code.

C

Carryback. A deduction or credit that cannot be employed on the current tax return, but which may be used to reduce taxable income or taxes payable in a prior year.

Carryforward. A deduction or credit that cannot be employed on the current tax return, but which may be used to reduce taxable income or taxes payable in a future year.

D

Deductible temporary difference. A temporary difference that will yield amounts that can be deducted in the future when determining taxable profit or loss.

Deferred tax asset. Income taxes that are recoverable in a future period.

Deferred tax liability. Income taxes payable in a future period.

I

Income tax. A tax that is based on the income of the party subject to the tax.

T

Tax position. A position taken in a tax return, which the filer uses to measure current or deferred income tax assets and liabilities. A tax position can yield a permanent reduction or deferral of income taxes payable.

Taxable income. A taxpayer's gross income, minus any allowable tax deductions.

Temporary difference. The difference between the carrying amount of an asset or liability in the balance sheet and its tax base.

V

Valuation allowance. A reserve that is used to offset the amount of a deferred tax asset.

Index

www.ingramcontent.com/pod-product-compliance
Lightning Source LLC
Chambersburg PA
CBHW051430200326
41520CB00023B/7425